THE 5-PARAGRAPH ESSAY MASTERY
A Teen Writer's Workbook

A WORKBOOK FOR TEENS, PROVIDING STEP-BY-STEP GUIDANCE ON HOW TO WRITE A 5-PARAGRAPH ESSAY

DR. FANATOMY

copyright@ dr. fanatomy 2024

All rights reserved. No part of this publication may be reproduced, distributed, or transmitted in any form or by any means, including photocopying, recording, or other electronic or mechanical methods, without the prior written permission of the publisher, except in the case of brief quotations embodied in critical reviews and certain other noncommercial uses permitted by copyright law.

This book is a work of non-fiction, and any resemblance to actual persons, living or dead, or actual events is purely coincidental.

The information and techniques described in this book are intended for educational and informational purposes only. The author and publisher shall not be held liable for any injury, damage, or loss arising from using or misusing the information presented in this book.

While every effort has been made to ensure the accuracy of the information contained within this book, the author and publisher make no warranties or representations express or implied, about the completeness, accuracy, reliability, suitability, or availability with respect to the contents of this book for any purpose. The use of any information provided in this book is at the reader's own risk.

Bonus Booklet For You!

With great pleasure, I warmly welcome you to purchase the book. Congratulations on stepping towards improving yourself and developing the skills necessary to thrive as a teenager and beyond.

Below is a surprise gift for you!

Download it from the link (or scan the QR code below)
https://bit.ly/TeeNavigationBonus

TABLE OF CONTENTS

1. **PREFACE: NAVIGATING YOUR WRITING JOURNEY** (Pg:4-6)

   - Welcome Message
   - Overview of the Workbook's Structure
   - How to Use This Workbook Effectively

2. **INTRODUCTION TO THE 5-PARAGRAPH ESSAY** (Pg:7-11)

   - Understanding the Basics
   - Importance of the 5-Paragraph Structure
   - Overview of the Writing Process
   - Activity Corner 1

3. **GETTING STARTED** (Pg:12-16)

   - Choosing a Topic
   - Crafting a Strong Thesis Statement
   - Practical example
   - Activity Corner 2

4. **THE BUILDING BLOCKS: PARAGRAPH STRUCTURE** (Pg:17-22)

   - Introduction to Paragraphs
   - Components of a Well-Structured Paragraph
   - Connecting Ideas with Smooth Transitions
   - Examples of essays for Teens
   - Activity Corner 3

5. **WRITING THE INTRODUCTION** (Pg: 23-30)

   - Hook, Line, and Thinker: Mastering the Introduction
   - Purpose and Significance of the Introduction
   - Formulating a Clear Thesis Statement
   - 5 Examples of Introduction
   - Activity Corner 4

6. BODY PARAGRAPHS: SUPPORTING YOUR IDEAS (Pg: 31-36)

- Setting the Stage - Topic Sentence
- Building the Excitement - Evidence
- Navigating the Twists - Analysis
- Seamless Transitions - The Safety Features
- Activity Corner 5

7. THE ART OF TRANSITIONS (Pg: 37-42)

- What Transitions Do
- How to Use Transitions
- Tips for Good Transitions
- Examples in Action
- Some More Examples
- Activity Corner 6

8. CRAFTING A CONVINCING CONCLUSION (Pg: 43-49)

- Importance of a Strong Conclusion
- How to Make Your Conclusion Awesome
- Examples in Action
- Activity Corner 7

9. REVISING AND EDITING (Pg: 50-55)

- The Revision Process: A Step-by-Step Guide
- Editing for Clarity, Grammar, and Style
- Activity Corner 8

10. PRACTICE MAKES PERFECT (Pg: 56-60)

- Essay Prompts for Practice
- Self-Evaluation and Reflection
- Peer Review Exercises
- Activity Corner 9

ACTIVITY ANSWERS (Pg: 61-68)

11. **TEN SAMPLE & TEN PRACTICE ESSAYS** (Pg: 69-109)

12. **PROMPT CHALLENGE** (Pg: 110-112)

CONCLUSION (Pg: 113)

1. Preface: Navigating Your Writing Journey

Welcome Message

Welcome to "The 5-Paragraph Essay Blueprint: A Teen Writer's Workbook"! This journey we're about to embark on is more than just a writing course; it's an opportunity to explore your creativity and learn to express your thoughts with clarity and purpose.

I want you to feel excited about the writing adventure ahead. Writing is a skill that continues to evolve with practice, and every word you put on paper is a step forward in your writing journey.

Overview of the Workbook's Structure:

Let's first take a moment to understand the layout of this workbook before we start discussing the details of essay writing. This isn't just a book you read; it's an interactive guide that will be your companion throughout your writing journey.

Section Breakdown:

- **Introduction:** Lay the foundation for understanding the 5-paragraph essay structure and its importance.

- **Body Chapters:** Each chapter focuses on a specific essay writing aspect, progressively building your skills.

- **Example Essays:** Refer to real-world examples to solidify your understanding.

- **Practical Exercises:** Engage in hands-on activities after each concept to reinforce your learning.

- **Reflection Spaces:** Throughout the workbook, find areas for personal reflection on your writing and progress.

How to Use This Workbook Effectively:

This workbook is your writing coach. Here's a guide on making the most of it:

- **Active Participation:** Approach each chapter with curiosity and a willingness to participate in exercises actively.

- **Personalization:** This workbook is your space. Scribble, doodle, and jot down thoughts. Make it uniquely yours.

- **Reflection:** Pause and reflect on your writing journey. Use the reflection spaces provided to assess your growth.

- **Consistency:** Building writing skills takes time. Dedicate consistent, focused time to each chapter for maximum impact.

- **Example Essay as Your Guide**: "The Power of Books" will be a practical example of effective essay writing. Refer back to it as you progress through the workbook.

As we embark on this writing journey together, remember that every word you write is progress, and every challenge you encounter is an opportunity to improve your writing skills.

Let's turn this writing journey into an exciting exploration of your unique voice and style.

Happy writing!

2. Introduction to the 5-Paragraph Essay

Understanding the Basics

Welcome to the foundational chapter of "The 5-Paragraph Essay Blueprint: A Teen Writer's Workbook." Here, we explore the quintessential 5-paragraph essay and its significance in shaping your writing prowess.

In essay writing, the 5-paragraph structure exemplifies clarity and organization. Let's break down its components:

- **Introduction (Paragraph 1):** This paragraph introduces the topic with a hook and concludes with a clear thesis statement, serving as a roadmap for the essay.

- **Body Paragraphs (Paragraphs 2,3,4):** Each body paragraph should present a supporting idea that reinforces the thesis, backed up with evidence, examples, and a logical flow.

- **Conclusion(Paragraph 5):** The conclusion is more than a summary. It encourages reflection on the narrative's significance.

Significance of the 5-Paragraph Structure:

Adhering to this format is valuable for teen writers as it provides a robust framework to articulate thoughts effectively. The 5-paragraph structure promotes clarity, organization, and concise expression - skills indispensable in communication.

Overview of the Writing Process

As we begin our essay writing journey, it is crucial to understand the writing process. It is not just about constructing sentences but a dynamic process of ideation, refinement, and eloquent expression.

Crafting "The Power of Books": A 5-Paragraph Blueprint:

Let's envision the exploration of the transformative influence of books in our example essay, "The Power of Books," unfolding through the following progression:

Introduction: Start with a captivating anecdote or thought-provoking quote about the enchantment of books. End with a thesis statement emphasizing literature's significant impact on personal growth.

Body Paragraphs:

- **Paragraph 1**: Explore how books serve as windows to diverse worlds, broadening perspectives and nurturing empathy.

- **Paragraph 2:** Dive into the role of books as mentors, offering guidance and solace during challenging times.

- **Paragraph 3:** Illuminate the power of books to spark creativity and intellectual curiosity.

Conclusion:

In this workbook, you will find practical exercises and insights to help you refine each element of your essay. The purpose is to help you create a masterpiece that reflects your unique voice and perspective.

As you progress through the workbook, you will discover how books can transform individuals and encourage contemplation on the importance of literature in our everyday lives.

Are you ready to begin the writing adventure and wield the power of the 5-paragraph essay?

Let's get started!

 ACTIVITY CORNER 1

Paragraph Puzzle: "Unscramble the Wisdom of Sports"

Objective:

Enhance your understanding of paragraph flow by rearranging the shuffled paragraphs to unveil the insightful essay **"How Sports Helps in Our Mental Wellbeing."**

Instructions:

Shuffle the Paragraphs:

- Below, you'll find five paragraphs from an essay on the mental benefits of sports. However, they are scrambled. Your task is to rearrange them in the correct order.

Unscramble the Wisdom:

- Analyze the content of each paragraph and consider how they might logically flow together. Rearrange the paragraphs to create a coherent and well-structured essay.

Reflect on Connections:

- Reflect on how each paragraph connects to the next as you unscramble the paragraphs. Consider the flow of ideas and the logical progression of the essay.

<u>Scrambled Paragraphs:</u>

(Paragraph A)
Sports contribute significantly to our mental well-being. Engaging in physical activities triggers the release of endorphins, the body's natural mood enhancers, positively impacting our mental state.

ACTIVITY CORNER 1

(Paragraph B)
Additionally, the camaraderie and social interactions fostered in sports environments create a sense of belonging and support, which is crucial in maintaining mental health.

(Paragraph C)
The positive effects of sports on mental health extend beyond the physical aspect. Regular exercise has been linked to reduced symptoms of anxiety and depression, promoting a more balanced and resilient mind.

(Paragraph D)
Exploring the connection between sports and mental well-being reveals a profound link between physical activity and psychological health. This connection is particularly evident in how sports reduce stress and improve mood.

(Paragraph E)
In conclusion, the holistic benefits of sports on mental health go beyond the physical realm. From stress reduction to enhanced mood and a sense of community, sports are vital in maintaining our overall mental well-being.

Your Task:
Unscramble and arrange the paragraphs correctly to unveil the essay's insights on "How Sports Helps in Our Mental Wellbeing."

Note: This exercise challenges your understanding of an essay's paragraph flow and logical sequencing. Enjoy the puzzle-solving process!

  **_Answer at the end_

3. Getting Started

Getting Started

Welcome to the process of launching your essay-writing journey! This chapter will guide you through crafting a 5-paragraph essay on the impact of social media on teenagers' mental well-being.

Choosing a Topic

Step 1: Explore Your Interests
Consider your interests; as a teenager, the digital world is a fascinating aspect of your life.

Step 2: Define Your Focus
Narrow down to a specific theme. Let's choose "The Influence of Social Media on Teenagers."

Step 3: Evaluate Relevance
Confirm that the theme aligns with current issues and concerns teenagers face today.

Brainstorming Ideas

Step 4: Freewriting
Set a timer and jot down thoughts. Consider aspects like the positive and negative effects of social media.

Step 5: Create Mind Maps
Visualize connections. Explore ideas like comparisons between different social media platforms and the role of parental guidance.

Step 6: Evaluate and Select
Choose the most compelling aspects for further exploration. Focus on the effects on mental health.

Crafting a Strong Thesis Statement

Step 7: Identify Key Points
After brainstorming ideas based on your chosen topic, identify critical points such as self-expression, connectivity, and potential risks.

Step 8: Formulate a Central Message
Teenagers use social media to express themselves and connect, but its impact on mental health and relationships requires examination.

Step 9: Refine
It is crucial to ensure that your thesis statement is clear and concise. Take some time to revise and make sure that it aligns well with the chosen topic to enhance its clarity.

- You have made progress toward writing an engaging essay by following the earlier steps.

- You have selected a topic related to the impact of social media on teenagers, explored different perspectives, and formulated a strong thesis statement.

- This initial work will pave the way for the remaining essay writing process. Therefore, continue to enjoy investigating the topic further!

Practical example :

Exploring an essay Topic: **"Balancing Screen Time for Teenagers"**

(a) Choosing a Topic

Step 1: *Explore Your Interests: As a teenager, your interests may revolve around technology and its impact on your daily life.*

Step 2: Define Your Focus: Narrow your broad interest to a specific theme, such as "Balancing Screen Time for Teenagers."

Step 3: Evaluate Relevance: Confirm that the theme aligns with current issues and concerns teenagers face in the digital age.

(b) Brainstorming Ideas

Step 4: Thoughts jot down: Set a timer and jot down thoughts on screen time's positive and negative effects on teenagers' well-being.

Step 5: Create Mind Maps: Visualize connections by exploring the benefits of limited screen time, potential risks of excessive use, and strategies for balance.

Step 6: Evaluate and select the most compelling aspects for further exploration, focusing on the mental health implications of screen time.

(c) Crafting a Strong Thesis Statement

Step 7: Identify Key Points: Based on your chosen topic and brainstormed ideas, identify critical points like the importance of balance and potential impacts on mental health.

Step 8: Formulate a Central Message: Create a concise statement reflecting your main idea: "While digital devices provide valuable resources, striking a balance in screen time is crucial for teenagers' mental well-being."

Step 9: Refine and Clarify: Ensure your thesis is clear and concise. Revise to enhance clarity and alignment with the chosen topic.

🎯 ACTIVITY CORNER 2

Prompt:

Match each topic below with its most suitable essay type. Then, craft a strong thesis statement that aligns with the chosen essay type.

Topics:

1. The Impact of Social Media on Body Image in Teens
2. The Benefits of Studying a Second Language
3. The Challenges of Growing Up in a Single-Parent Household
4. The Ethical Debate Surrounding Artificial Intelligence
5. The Role of Music in Shaping Cultural Identity

Essay Types:

- Persuasive
- Analytical
- Explanatory

**Answer at the end

4. The Building Blocks: Paragraph Structure

The Building Blocks: Paragraph Structure

Imagine your essay as a magnificent castle. Your thesis statement is like the imposing tower, but you need more than just that. Think of each paragraph as a vital brick that forms the walls, buildings, and walkways that bring your castle to life. To construct effective paragraphs, let's dive into some secrets of paragraph construction. that. Think of each paragraph as a vital brick that forms the walls, buildings, and walkways that bring your castle to life. To construct effective paragraphs, let's dive into some secrets of paragraph construction.

Introduction to Paragraphs:

Have you ever experienced those uncomfortable pauses during a conversation when you use words like "um" and "ah"?

Well, paragraphs are the complete opposite of that. They are like mini-conversations inside your writing, each with a specific subject and a clear message. They function like stepping stones across a river, guiding your reader smoothly and logically from one point to the next.

Components of a Well-Structured Paragraph:

Each paragraph is like a mini-essay with an introduction, body, and conclusion. Therefore, every paragraph should contain:

Topic Sentence:

- *Example: In a discussion about the impact of social media on friendships, your topic sentence could be: "Contrary to popular belief, social media can strengthen, rather than weaken, meaningful connections."*

Supporting Evidence:

- *Example: Present statistics or studies showing how online communication has facilitated global friendships and connected people across distances.*

Analysis and Explanation:

- *For example, could you explain why this evidence is significant? Discuss how virtual connections allow individuals to share experiences and perspectives, fostering a sense of camaraderie.*

Concluding Sentence:

- *Example: Conclude the paragraph by summarizing the main point or teasing what's coming next: "By understanding the positive aspects of social media, we can harness its potential to cultivate genuine and lasting friendships."*

Connecting Ideas with Smooth Transitions:

Picture yourself jumping from one rock to another while crossing a stream. You might splash your face or lose balance if the rocks are too far apart.

Similarly, transitions act as stepping stones between paragraphs, seamlessly connecting ideas and guiding your reader along the path of your essay.

Here are some transition words and phrases for different purposes:

- ***Adding to an idea***: *moreover, additionally, besides, also*
- ***Showing contrast***: *however, nevertheless, on the other hand, despite*
- ***Explaining cause and effect***: *therefore, consequently, hence, as a result*
- ***Summarizing:*** *in conclusion, to sum up, finally, overall*

Examples essays for Teens:

Let's say you're writing an essay about the *impact of video games on learning*. Here's how a paragraph might look:

Topic Sentence:

"While some may argue that video games are mindless distractions, research suggests they can enhance cognitive skills like memory and problem-solving."

Supporting Evidence:

A recent study showed that playing puzzle games can improve recall speed by 20%. Moreover, action games require quick thinking and strategic planning, valuable skills in real-world challenges.

Analysis and Explanation:

This doesn't mean that every game is beneficial for brain development. Violent or repetitive games can have adverse effects. However, if chosen wisely, video games can be a fun and interactive way to enhance mental agility.

Concluding Sentence:

Understanding the structure of paragraphs and using transitions effectively can significantly improve the quality of your essays. It lets you showcase your ideas with clarity and power, turning your writing from shaky bridges to sturdy castles.

So, the next time you pick up your controller, remember that you are not just killing dragons but also potentially conquering mental challenges. It's important to remember that practice makes perfect, so grab your pen or keyboard, experiment with different paragraph structures, and watch your writing skills skyrocket!

Remember, this is just a starting point, so feel free to add more examples based on your interests and the topics you might be writing about. Have fun building those essay castles!

🎯 ACTIVITY CORNER 3

Paragraph Puzzle Palace!

Challenge:

You've conquered the basics of paragraph structure; now put your skills to the test! Below, you'll find three scrambled paragraphs related to a fictional teen movie about a time-traveling robot. Each paragraph lacks proper order and transition words. Unscramble them, identify the missing transitions, and choose the best options to connect the ideas smoothly. Finally, write the corrected paragraph with transitions in the space provided.

Paragraph 1 (Scrambled):

- Sarah squinted at the chrome contraption, its metallic claws gleaming under the disco ball's light.
- Suddenly, the robot whirred to life, sparks leaping from its joints.
- Panic surged through her veins. What was this malfunctioning machine doing in her bedroom?
- A disembodied voice echoed, "Greetings, Sarah. I am Zorr, a time-traveling robot from the year 2247."

Paragraph 2 (Scrambled):

- Time travel? This had to be a joke.
- Zorr unfolded a holographic screen, displaying images of a futuristic cityscape bathed in neon lights.
- "Your world is in danger," the robot declared, his voice surprisingly gentle.
- Sarah's mind reeled. A time-traveling robot, a futuristic mission, danger… was this real?

🎯 ACTIVITY CORNER 3

Paragraph 3 (Scrambled):

- "But I'm just a normal teenager!" she blurted, feeling a mix of fear and excitement.
- "You are the chosen one," Zorr insisted, his gaze unwavering.
- "A prophecy foretold that..." His words were cut short by a loud crash from downstairs.
- Sarah and Zorr exchanged startled glances. This was just the beginning.

Missing Transitions:

- Between Paragraph 1 and 2: (a) Meanwhile, (b) Consequently, (c) In that instant,
- Between Paragraph 2 and 3: (a) Sarah braced herself, (b) With a sigh of disbelief, (c) Yet, despite her doubts,

**Answer at the end

5. Writing the Introduction

Hook, Line, and Thinker: Mastering the Introduction

Imagine your essay as a delicious sandwich. The introduction is like the first bite that either entices you to keep going or makes you put down the sandwich altogether. If the introduction is bland and boring, it won't grab your attention, but if it's full of flavor, intrigue, and ideas, you'll be eager to devour the rest! This chapter provides you with the necessary tools to make your introductions irresistible, hook your readers, and set the stage for a stellar essay.

Purpose and Significance of the Introduction:

Imagine entering a movie theater with a blindfold; you wouldn't know the plot, characters, or genre. The same is true for your essay without a strong introduction. Its purpose is to:

- **Grab attention**: It's your chance to say "Hey, look at me!" and pique the reader's curiosity. Think of it like a trailer for your essay, giving a glimpse of the exciting ideas and arguments to come.

- **Introduce the topic**: Clearly state what your essay is about, giving the reader a roadmap of the key points you'll be exploring.

- **Present your thesis statement**: This is your central argument, the "big idea" of your essay. The introduction prepares the reader to understand and engage with your unique perspective.

Crafting an Engaging Hook:

Think of your hook as the bait on your fishing line. It needs to grab the reader's attention and make them want to know more. Here are some strategies:

- Start with a surprising fact or statistic: Did you know dogs can sniff out cancer with incredible accuracy? This is a great way to engage readers in your essay about animal intelligence.

- Ask a thought-provoking question: What if social media could inspire kindness?

- Use vivid language and imagery: Let your words paint a picture! Describe the vibrant energy of a music festival or the tranquil wonder of gazing at a starry night sky.

- Share a personal anecdote: Tell a story about your experience to help readers connect and get invested in your essay.

Formulating a Clear Thesis Statement:

Think of your thesis statement as the compass guiding your essay. It should be:

- **Specific**: "Please ensure that your topic is narrow enough but has a clear and focused argument with a specific stance. For instance, instead of stating that "Social media is important," it is better to say, "While social media has benefits for connection, its emphasis on curated online personas ultimately harms self-esteem and authentic relationships."

- **Debatable**: Your thesis should be thought-provoking, inviting exploration and discussion from the reader rather than stating a universally accepted fact.

- **Relevant**: Your thesis should be thought-provoking, not a widely accepted fact, to spark discussion and exploration of your perspective.

Writing a captivating introduction is a skill that takes time and practice. Don't be afraid to experiment with different hooks and thesis statements until you find the one that best fits your essay.

By mastering the technique of writing a great introduction, you can make your essays stand out and grab the attention of your readers from the very beginning. That's why it's important for writers to aim for creating a hook that will engage their readers and showcase the power of their words.!

Bonus Tip: After you finish writing your introduction, it's a good idea to read it out loud. This will help you determine if the introduction is smooth and engaging.

If it's not, feel free to revise it until it becomes genuinely compelling! This chapter offers practical examples and straightforward advice to assist your students in creating captivating introductions that set the stage for powerful essays. Happy writing!

Remember:

- Keep your introduction concise and engaging, aiming for no more than a few paragraphs.

- Please make sure your hook and thesis statement are directly connected, with the hook sparking curiosity and the thesis providing a clear roadmap for your argument.

- Don't shy away from taking a specific stance on the topic, encouraging your reader to engage with your unique perspective.

A powerful introduction can transform an essay from a mere collection of words into a compelling narrative. Aspiring writers should use their voices to explore social media's intriguing and complex world and its impact on our social connections.

5 Examples of Introduction

1. Topic: Conquering Test Anxiety (Hook, Line, and Thinker)

Hook: Are you experiencing butterflies in your stomach, your brain turning into mush, and your palms sweating like a leaky faucet? Test anxiety hits everyone, but what if I told you you can tame that beast and ace your exams?

Line: This essay dives into the science of test anxiety, revealing its secrets and offering battle-tested strategies to silence the inner freak-out and boost your confidence.

Thinker: Forget cram sessions and lucky charms; we're unlocking the power of mindfulness, breathing techniques, and study hacks to transform test anxiety from a monster to a manageable (and even conquerable) foe.

2. Topic: The Power of Music (Hook, Line, and Thinker)

Hook: Have you ever heard a song that makes you want to dance like nobody's watching? Or a melody that gives you chills? I get it! That's because music is more than just noise; it's a superpower that can touch your soul.

Line: This essay examines the scientific impact of music on our brains, emotions, and social connections, exploring its magical properties.

Thinker: From catchy pop tunes to soul-stirring symphonies, we'll uncover the secret language of music and its ability to unite, inspire, and even heal. Get ready to crank up the volume on your understanding of this incredible art form!

3. Topic: Embracing Imperfections (Hook, Line, and Thinker)

Hook: Filter fail, social media envy, the pressure to be perfect... it's enough to make you want to crawl under a rock. But guess what? Nobody's perfect, and that's okay!

Line: This essay celebrates the beauty of imperfections, exploring how embracing our quirks, flaws, and vulnerabilities can make us stronger, more relatable, and, ultimately, happier.

Thinker: Forget the airbrushed selfies and unrealistic expectations; we're rewriting the definition of "perfect" to include messy hair, bad jokes, and all the glorious weirdness that makes us unique. Get ready to flaunt your flaws and unleash your inner awesome!

4. Topic: The Art of Saying No (Hook, Line, and Thinker)

- Hook: Feeling like a human calendar, juggling endless requests and obligations? Sometimes, the most powerful word you can learn is "no."

Line: This essay explores the importance of setting boundaries and the liberating power of saying no. We'll learn how to prioritize your needs, avoid burnout, and reclaim time and energy control.

Thinker: Forget about "people pleasing" and guilt trips; we're learning to say "no" with confidence and grace, protecting our precious time and mental space for what truly matters. Get ready to ditch the FOMO and embrace the "JOMO" (joy of missing out) on things that don't serve you!

5. Topic: The Magic of Travel (Hook, Line, and Thinker)

Hook: Have you ever dreamt of scaling mountains in Nepal, diving into coral reefs in Fiji, or wandering the markets of Morocco? Travel isn't just about selfies and souvenirs; it's an adventure for the soul!

Line: This essay explores the transformative power of travel, opening our minds to new cultures, perspectives, and possibilities. We'll discover how stepping outside our comfort zones can lead to self-discovery, personal growth, and unforgettable experiences.

Thinker: Forget the tourist traps and Instagrammable moments; we're diving into the authentic heart of travel, embracing the unexpected, the uncomfortable, and the utterly breathtaking. Prepare to pack your bags for a journey that will change you forever!

Keep in mind:

- When writing an introduction for an essay or any piece of writing, it is important to keep it brief yet interesting, limiting it to only a few paragraphs.

- The hook, which is the opening sentence, should be captivating and ignite the reader's curiosity. Moreover, the thesis statement should be linked to the hook and provide a clear direction for the essay's argument.

- Therefore, it is essential to take a firm and unambiguous stance on the topic, allowing the reader to engage with the author's unique point of view.

ACTIVITY CORNER 4

Matchmaker: Find Your Intro Style!

Match the following intro styles to the examples below:

Intro Styles:

1. **The Storyteller:** Weaves a personal narrative, drawing readers into your experience and connecting it to your main point.
2. **The Question Master:** Poses a thought-provoking question that sparks curiosity and sets the stage for exploration.
3. **The Fact Pro:** Drops a mind-blowing fact or statistic that grabs attention and highlights the significance of your topic.
4. **The Scene Setter:** Paints a vivid picture, immersing readers in the world of your essay and establishing the tone.
5. **The Quote Connoisseur:** Uses a powerful quote to introduce your theme, providing depth and authority from the outset.

Essay Excerpts:

A. "Remember the dusty box of childhood photos you stumbled upon? Faded smiles, forgotten holidays, faces both familiar and strange. Those memories, hidden in cardboard vaults, whisper tales of who we were and who we've become. This essay delves into the power of nostalgia, exploring how our past shapes us, haunts us, and ultimately guides us towards our future."

B. "Is social media a gateway to connection or a breeding ground for loneliness? It's a question that keeps millions scrolling, comparing, and questioning their reality. This essay dives into the complex relationship between social media and our social well-being, analyzing its potential to bridge divides or build walls, to spark joy or fuel isolation."

C. "Did you know the average person spends 7 years of their life watching cat videos online? And while feline acrobatics are undeniably entertaining, perhaps it's time we questioned the impact of an attention-grabbing, dopamine-fueled digital world. This essay examines the changing landscape of information consumption, exploring the consequences of our online habits and calling for a mindful approach to navigating the digital ocean."

D. "Imagine stepping off a bustling city street and into a vibrant rainforest, the air thick with the scent of damp earth and the sounds of exotic birdsong. This is the feeling of traveling beyond your comfort zone, of immersing yourself in the unknown and expanding your worldview. This essay celebrates the transformative power of travel, its ability to challenge our expectations, ignite our curiosity, and reveal the interconnectedness of our planet."

E. "In the words of Maya Angelou, 'There is no greater agony than bearing an untold story inside you.' This essay echoes that sentiment, exploring the importance of expressing ourselves, sharing our unique narratives, and finding our voice in a world that often demands silence. From whispered secrets to public proclamations, we'll delve into the transformative power of storytelling and its ability to connect us, heal us, and shape our lives."

Ready to match?

This activity aims to help students discover the introduction style that best suits their writing voice and the topic they have chosen. It is important to keep in mind that there is no one-size-fits-all approach, and students should feel free to embrace their creativity when crafting their introduction.

By using real-world examples and matching them to the different styles, students can gain a better understanding of how each approach works and experiment with incorporating it into their own writing. I hope that this activity proves to be helpful in identifying the perfect intro match for your students!

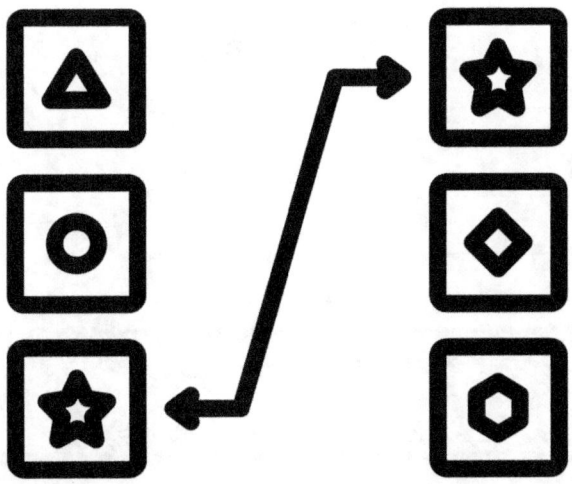

6. Body Paragraphs: Supporting Your Ideas

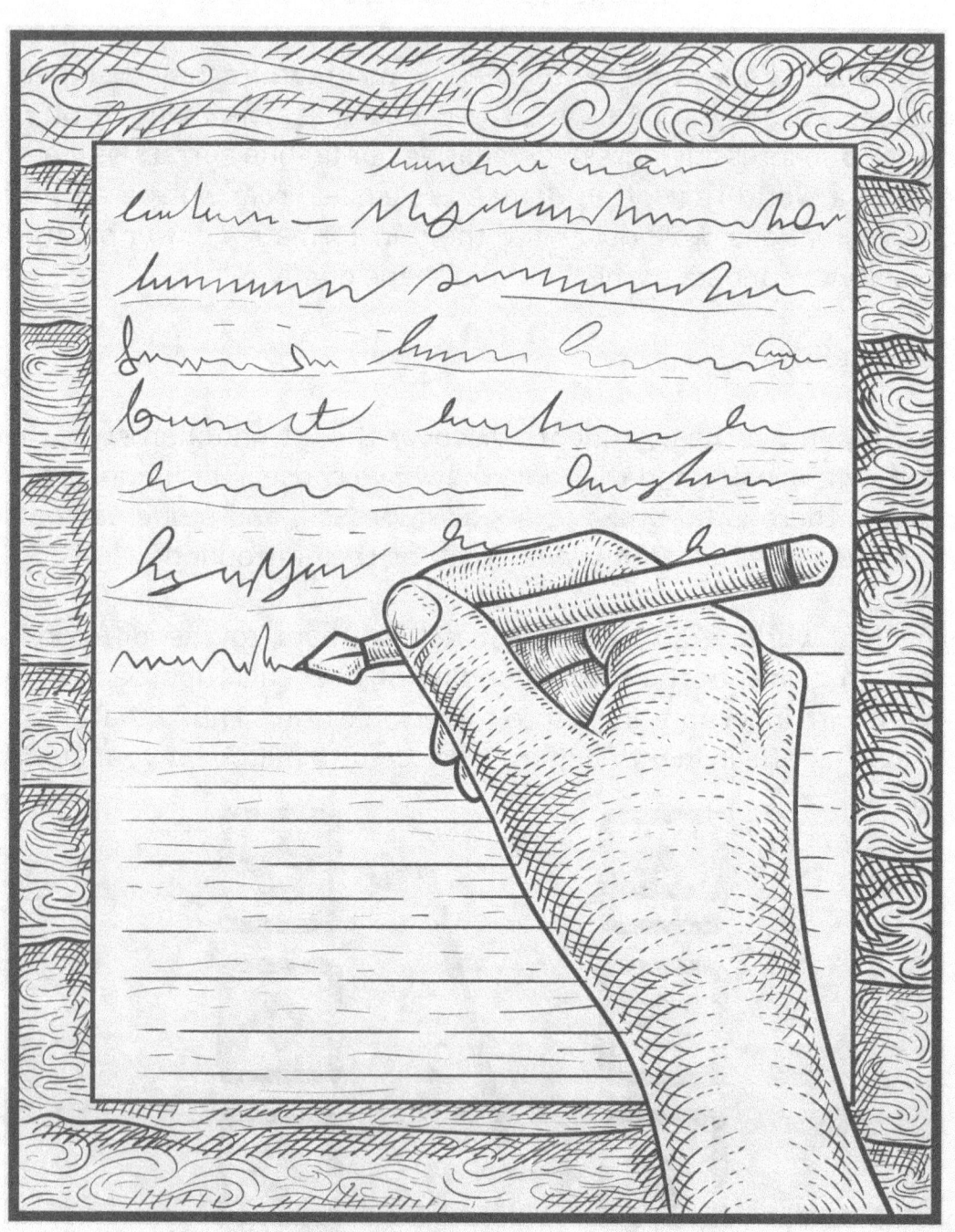

Imagine your essay as an exhilarating rollercoaster ride filled with unexpected twists, turns, and exciting drops. The introduction acts as the entrance that invites readers into the park of your ideas. However, the loops and corkscrews offered in each body paragraph keep readers engaged and thrilled throughout the journey.

Each of these paragraphs offers a new perspective, supported by evidence and analysis that captivates the reader. These captivating loops leave your readers craving more excitement. So, how do you construct such captivating loops that keep your readers engaged throughout the essay?

Step 1: Setting the Stage - Topic Sentence

Envision each paragraph of your essay as a neon sign that illuminates the night sky. Each paragraph needs to have a catchy slogan: your topic sentence. The topic sentence should proclaim, "Get ready for an amazing experience!" and hint at the exciting ride ahead.

For instance, if your essay advocates for longer school lunch breaks, your focus on increased focus could be introduced with a topic sentence like this: "Energizing Minds, Beyond Just Satisfying Hunger: Extended lunch breaks aren't merely a feast; they're a power-up for students' attention and academic success."

Step 2: Building the Excitement - Evidence

Imagine a rollercoaster that appears to be built in mid-air - that wouldn't be very scary, would it? Similarly, your paragraphs need strong evidence to support them, much like sturdy steel tracks that anchor the most thrilling loops. You can use facts, statistics, research, and exciting examples as thrill-building materials to make your writing more interesting and engaging.

Facts: Have you ever heard that NASA found astronauts' focus improved by 25% after a proper meal? Now, imagine the impact on students facing challenging exams!

Statistics: According to a survey of 500 high schoolers, 80% felt more focused and ready to learn after an extended lunch break compared to only 20% during the usual short break.

Research: An academic paper in the Journal of Education argues that longer lunch breaks enhance cognitive function, reduce stress, and improve memory retention and problem-solving skills.

Real-world example: Green Valley High School in California adopted a 90-minute lunch break, and the results were astonishing – their test scores soared, proving that refreshing breaks fuel academic success.

Remember, variety adds spice to the ride! Mix and match these evidence types to keep your loops exciting, steering clear of repetitive flat sections that might make readers lose interest.

Step 3: Navigating the Twists - Analysis

Imagine riding a rollercoaster straight up without sharp turns at the top. It's just a dull, uphill climb. When writing an essay, your analysis is critical in explaining how your chosen evidence connects to your arguments.

This helps your readers understand and appreciate your point of view. For example, if you're writing an essay about the benefits of longer lunch breaks for students, you could analyze a NASA study showing how proper lunch nutrition can help students maintain their cognitive capacity and avoid mental fatigue.

Through this analysis, you demonstrate your ability to think critically and make connections between different pieces of information. This shows you're not just throwing random facts into your essay without thought or purpose.

Step 4: Seamless Transitions - The Safety Features

Imagine riding a rollercoaster without safety bars - not exactly confidence-inspiring!

Transition words and phrases serve as signposts, guiding readers through loops seamlessly without feeling lost.

- **For comparison**, however, similarly, on the other hand
- **For illustration**: for example, in fact, such as
- **For emphasis**: therefore, consequently, hence
- **For continuation**: moreover furthermore, besides

These words serve as friendly park attendants, guiding readers through your essay's thrilling twists and turns with clarity and safety.

Keep in mind:

- When writing an essay, you should structure each body paragraph like a unique loop focusing on a single point related to your central thesis. This approach is similar to a cart hurtling through the twists of a rollercoaster.

- To make your essay more compelling, use diverse evidence and analysis to keep your loops thrilling and your arguments airtight. Employing transition words to ensure a smooth ride through your essay's thrilling journey is also important.

- Lastly, proofread and refine your loops, ensuring clarity, conciseness, and a logical flow that excites your readers. By following these guidelines, you can create an essay that is both engaging and easy to follow.

ACTIVITY CORNER 5

Mystery Essay Matchmaker: Unmasking the Body Paragraphs!

Imagine your essay as a detective novel. The introduction sets the stage, introduces the characters (ideas!), and plunges you into a perplexing mystery.

But what do you think about the body paragraphs? They contain the crucial clues, the evidence that will lead you to the truth (your thesis!).

Can you correctly match the appropriate bodies with the appropriate introductions? It's time to wear your detective cap and become the ultimate Essay Matchmaker!

Challenge:

- Four mysterious introductions and five intriguing body paragraphs are given below.

- Your task is to match each introduction with its corresponding body paragraph.

- You should consider each introduction's tone, theme, and critical points to find its perfect match with a body paragraph.

- Use your detective skills to piece together the clues and solve the puzzle.

Intros:

1. *As you enter the dimly lit antique shop, a shiver of anticipation creeps down your spine. Dust motes dance in the fractured sunlight, each one a whispering secret from the past. What treasures lie hidden among these shelves, waiting to tell their stories? This essay delves into the captivating allure of antiques and their power to transport us to bygone eras and connect us to the whispers of history.*

2. *The rhythmic click-clack of keyboards fills the air, a symphony of digital creativity. In the sprawling world of online gaming, millions gather, forging alliances, conquering challenges, and building virtual empires. But is this world just a mindless escape, or does it hold the potential for real-world connection and growth? This essay explores the complex role of online gaming in our society, examining its challenges and unexpected benefits.*

3. The aroma of freshly baked bread hangs heavy in the air, a comforting promise of warmth and nourishment. Food is not just fuel but a language of love, culture, and community. This essay embarks on a culinary journey, exploring the power of food to connect us to our heritage, celebrate traditions, and weave the threads of shared experiences across generations.

4. Silence reigns in the vast expanse of the library, broken only by the gentle turning of pages. Within these towering shelves lie countless universes waiting to be unraveled. But what happens when the lines between fiction and reality blur? This essay examines the transformative power of reading and its ability to transport us to imaginary worlds and shape our understanding of ourselves and the world around us.

Body Paragraphs:

A. In a recent study, researchers found that online gamers often exhibit enhanced communication and teamwork skills honed through their collaborative efforts in virtual landscapes. These skills can translate into real-world benefits, strengthening relationships and increased employability.

B. The ancient Egyptians believed certain foods held the power of gods and goddesses, offering them as sacred offerings and consuming them to imbibe their divine qualities. This deep connection between food and belief highlights its role as a bridge between the physical and the spiritual.

C. Stepping into a vintage shop is like stepping into a time machine. You might stumble upon a flapper dress from the roaring twenties, a chipped teacup whispering tales of Victorian tea parties, or a dusty gramophone promising forgotten melodies. Each object is a tangible link to the past, a silent storyteller waiting to be heard.

D. A well-crafted story can reshape our perspectives, challenging our assumptions and pushing us to see the world through new eyes. As we journey alongside fictional characters, we confront their struggles, celebrate their triumphs, and ultimately, reflect on our lives with newfound empathy and understanding.

E. Baking bread is an act of creation, transforming simple ingredients into something warm, fragrant, and nourishing. It fosters a sense of community as the aroma fills the house and brings loved ones together to share the fruits of this culinary alchemy.

7. The Art of Transitions

Imagine your essay as a group of extraordinary islands in a vast ocean. Each island, that is, each paragraph, is full of fantastic ideas, evidence, and cool stuff. However, how can you move from one island to the next without getting lost in the waves?

That's where transitions come in handy, like bridges, guiding you smoothly from one point to the next, thus making your essay flow like a chill current instead of a bumpy ride.

What Transitions Do:

Think of transitions as your essay's tour guides.

They:

- **Show connections**: Like signs pointing the way, they tell how your current point connects to the one before and the next one.
- **Keep things smooth**: They stop your ideas from jumping around too much, making your essay easy to read.
- **Highlight important stuff**: They can point out the excellent parts of your argument so your readers can experience them.
- **Keep it interesting**: Transitions make your essay fun to read, like adding sprinkles to ice cream.

How to Use Transitions:

Let's build those bridges! Here are some excellent transition words for different things:

- To compare: however, similarly, on the other hand, in contrast
- To give examples: for example, in fact, such as
- To emphasize: therefore, consequently, hence
- To keep going: moreover furthermore, besides
- To show time: firstly, secondly, next, finally
- To explain cause and effect: because, so, thus, as a result

Remember: Limit transitions, as excessive use can spoil the quality.

Tips for Good Transitions:

To use transitions like a pro, here are some tips:

- **Talk naturally**: Pretend you're talking to a friend, not giving a speech.
- **Switch it up**: Don't always use the same transitions – keep it interesting.
- **Match your words**: Use transitions that fit with what you're talking about.
- **Read out loud**: Listen to how your essay sounds and change transitions if necessary.

Examples in Action:

Let's see how transitions work in an actual essay:

Topic: Why we need longer school lunch breaks

- Paragraph 1: School is stressful, with packed schedules. Lunch, however, should be a smooth refueling stop. (Transition: however, shows a difference)

- Paragraph 2: Studies prove that longer lunch breaks help our brains. For example, a study found that students with 90-minute lunch breaks had better attention and test scores. (Transition: for instance, gives actual proof)

- Paragraph 3: So, longer lunch breaks aren't just about giving students a break – they boost our grades and make us feel better. (Transition: so shows a result)

See how transitions make the essay easy to follow?

Challenge:

Write a short paragraph about your favorite hobby or activity. Use at least two transitions to show how different parts of your hobby connect. Share it with a friend and see if they can spot your cool transitions!

Keep in mind

Transitions are like the secret heroes of your essay. Use them well, and your writing will flow smoothly, taking your readers on a fun journey from start to finish.

Some More Examples :

- **Paragraph 1**: Binge-watching your favorite show might seem like the ultimate relaxation, but *in contrast*, research shows it can lead to increased anxiety and difficulty focusing. *Similarly*, staying glued to your phone before bed disrupts sleep patterns and makes you groggy in the morning. (Transition: "in contrast" and "similarly" highlight a comparison between different activities with adverse effects.)

- **Paragraph 2**: *On the other hand*, learning a new instrument boosts cognitive function and improves memory. *Furthermore*, it fosters creativity and provides a sense of accomplishment, boosting self-esteem and confidence. (Transition: "On the other hand," introduces a contrasting positive effect, and "furthermore" adds another benefit to strengthen the positive argument.)

- **Paragraph 3:** Crafting the perfect social media post might seem like a harmless way to express yourself, but it can also lead to unhealthy comparisons and feelings of inadequacy. *However*, face-to-face interactions with friends and family foster genuine connections and build stronger relationships. *Moreover*, research shows that in-person social interaction releases hormones that reduce stress and boost happiness.

- **Paragraph 4:** Some argue that video games waste time, distract students from schoolwork, and promote a sedentary lifestyle. *On the contrary*, certain video games can enhance problem-solving skills, strategic thinking, and even hand-eye coordination. *In fact*, studies have shown that strategic video games can improve cognitive flexibility and memory.

🎯 ACTIVITY CORNER 6

Transition Time Machine: Fill in the Blanks and Navigate Your Essay!

Remember those handy time machines from sci-fi movies? Well, imagine your transitions are time machines for your essay, transporting your reader smoothly from one point to the next. In this fill-in-the-blank activity, you'll be the master pilot, guiding your readers through your ideas with the perfect transition choices!

1. Time Warp to Contrast:

You're arguing for longer school breaks. Fill in the blank to seamlessly transition from highlighting the adverse effects of short breaks to the benefits of longer ones:

The current system often leaves students feeling stressed and overwhelmed. (___), longer breaks could provide much-needed mental and physical rejuvenation, improving focus and academic performance.

(a) Therefore, (b) In contrast, (c) Consequently, (d) For example,

2. Zoom Forward to Illustration:

You're writing about the power of music. Use the blank to transition from stating its general impact to providing a specific example:

Music has the unique ability to evoke emotions and memories like nothing else. (___), a song like Queen's "Bohemian Rhapsody" can transport you back to a childhood summer spent by the beach, with the smell of sunscreen and the sound of crashing waves.

(a) For instance, (b) Moreover, (c) Likewise, (d) Hence,

3. Flashback to Emphasis:

You're advocating for sustainable fashion choices. Use the blank to emphasize the urgency of the issue after detailing the harmful effects of fast fashion:

The environmental and ethical costs of fast fashion are undeniable. (___), we can't simply ignore these consequences and continue wearing clothes at our planet's and people's expense.

(a) As a result, (b) Clearly, (c) Similarly, (d) On the other hand,

4. Fast Forward to Time Sequence:

You're writing about the evolution of technology. Use the blank to transition from discussing early inventions to the rapid advancements of today:

The bulky transistors of the first computers seem almost comical compared to the sleek smartphones we carry today. (___), technological innovation has accelerated exponentially, blurring the lines between reality and what was once science fiction.

(a) In fact, (b) Secondly, (c) In contrast, (d) Next,

5. Rewind to Cause and Effect:

You're explaining the importance of reading. Use the blank to connect the act of reading to its impact on a person's worldview:

Immersing yourself in different stories and perspectives expands your understanding of the world beyond your experiences. (___), reading can challenge your assumptions, cultivate empathy, and make you a more open-minded and informed.

(a) Hence, (b) Similarly, (c) Because, (d) For example,

8. Crafting a Convincing Conclusion

Have you ever watched a movie that left you feeling emotional or deep in thought? Believe it or not, your essays can have the same effect on your readers! The conclusion is the final touch that can make your essay stand out and leave a lasting impression.

In this guide, we will explore how to craft a conclusion that is not just a summary but will make your readers go "Wow!" - just like the final chord of a rock song. Remember those movie endings that leave you cheering, crying, or lost in thought?

Your essays can do that, too! The conclusion is like the grand finale, the last touch that makes your readers go, "Wow!" Let's explore how to craft a decision that's not just a summary but leaves a lasting impression, like the final chord of a rock song.

Why a Strong Conclusion Matters:

Consider the conclusion of the final bite of a delicious meal, leaving you satisfied and wanting more. A solid conclusion does the same thing:

- Recaps your main points: It summarizes your main arguments and evidence like a quick reminder of the best parts.
- Leaves a lasting impression: It adds a final punch – a call to action, a thought-provoking question, or something that keeps your reader thinking.
- Solidifies your argument: It ties everything together, showing why your perspective matters.

How to Make Your Conclusion Awesome:
Here are some tips to make your conclusion stand out:

- No repeats: Instead of restating your thesis, provide a new perspective that complements it.

- Beyond summary: Adding a final layer of insight to a summary is like providing commentary that explains why your essay matters.

- Hit the emotions: Adding an anecdote, a powerful quote, or an image can evoke emotions and add depth to your writing.

- Call to action: Challenge your reader to think or act differently. Ask a question, suggest more research, or urge for change – like the final inspiring chorus of a protest song.

- Leave them wanting more: End on a strong note – a thought-provoking idea or a surprising twist. It's like the perfect closing riff that makes you want an encore.

Examples in Action:

Let's see how these techniques work in real-life conclusions:

- Topic: Arguing for longer school lunch breaks

Conclusion: The next time someone says a more extended lunch break is a waste, remember – it's an investment. It's investing in our well-being, our focus, and our success. Let's stop treating lunch like a pit stop and start making it the power boost it deserves. A well-rested, well-fed mind is ready to conquer the world.

- Topic: Exploring the power of reading

Conclusion: As we close this book, remember that stories aren't just ink on paper. They're doorways to new worlds, mirrors reflecting our own, and compasses guiding us. Keep reading, keep learning, and keep your mind wide open – because within the pages of a book lies the potential to become anything you dream of and more.

Challenge:

Revise your favorite movie, song, or book conclusion for impact and memorability. Share it with a friend and watch them cheer!

Remember:

Your conclusion is the final opportunity for you to make a lasting impression on your reader. Therefore, it is essential to put in the effort to create a powerful and effective conclusion.

You can achieve this by using strong language, evoking emotions, and leaving your readers with something to think about long after reading your text. With practice, you can master the art of crafting conclusions that rival even the most epic grand finales!

One more example

Imagine that you have written an essay advocating for later school start times. In your essay, you have presented research on the significance of sleep for teenagers, highlighted the disadvantages of early mornings, and offered solutions such as adjusting bus schedules. Now, it is time to conclude your essay with a grand finale.

Option 1: The Thought-Provoker:

"When you see a tired, zombie-eyed teenager dragging themselves to class before sunrise, it's important to understand that it's not just laziness. Their biology is fighting against an unnatural schedule. We wouldn't ask athletes to compete on zero sleep, so why do we expect students to learn the same way? It may be time to reconsider forcing teenagers to be early birds and allow them to function as night owls when their brains are best prepared to learn and absorb information."

This option:

- Uses relatable imagery of "zombie-eyed teenagers" to grab attention.

- Frames the problem as a fight for biological needs, adding weight to the argument.

- Ends with a powerful metaphor of "night owls" taking flight, leaving a positive and memorable image.

Option 2: The Call to Action:

"Envision a classroom filled with focused, well-rested students and at their cognitive best. Think of a world where students experience fewer headaches, better moods, and can achieve their full learning potential. This isn't a mere daydream but a tangible future that can be achieved by a simple adjustment in school start times. Rather than fighting the dawn, let's work together to make a positive change. Let's advocate for teenagers, for science, and for a brighter future where sleep is considered an ally and a fuel for academic excellence. Who else is in?"

This option:

- Creates a vivid picture of the desired outcome, appealing to the reader's emotions.

- Connects the argument to academic success, making it relevant to teenage concerns.

- Ends with a solid call to action, inviting the reader to participate in the change.

Both options have a significant impact but do so in distinct ways. You should choose the option that fits your essay's tone and the impact you want to leave on the reader.

Remember, a great conclusion is like a fireworks display - it ignites a spark in the reader's mind that lasts long after reading. Don't be afraid to experiment, have fun, and let your creativity shine

ACTIVITY CORNER 7

Practice Exercise: Conclude with Confidence!

Scenario:

You've written an essay arguing for stricter regulations on social media platforms to combat cyberbullying. You've presented research on the harmful effects of cyberbullying, highlighted the limitations of current self-moderation systems, and offered specific solutions like mandatory reporting systems and age verification tools. Now, it's time to craft your conclusion!

Choose the **BEST** option for a concluding paragraph based on the essay's content and the tips provided in the chapter.

Option 1:

In conclusion, cyberbullying is a serious issue plaguing online communities, significantly impacting teenagers. We must hold social media platforms accountable and demand stricter regulations to create a safer digital environment. Therefore, we need stricter reporting systems, age verification tools, and harsher penalties for offenders. Remember, the internet may be vast, but our responsibility to protect each other shouldn't be.

Option 2:

The next time you scroll through your social media feed, consider the hidden realities behind the filtered selfies and witty captions.

Cyberbullying exists in the shadows, leaving scars that linger long after the screen fades dark. We, as users and citizens, have the power to demand change. Let's urge social media giants to rise above their algorithms and prioritize human well-being. It's time to turn the tide on cyberbullying and build a brighter, more compassionate online world.

Option 3:

Cyberbullying isn't just a digital problem – it's a reflection of the values we choose to uphold in our virtual communities. The anonymity of the internet emboldens some to spew venom while others remain silent observers. But silence isn't neutrality; it's complicity. Let's choose to be active allies, to report violations, and to speak out against cruelty. Our collective voice can drown out the whispers of hate and build a digital landscape where kindness reigns supreme.

9. Revising and Editing

Do you ever look at your essay and feel like it's a cold pizza left out for too long? It's unappealing, has toppings you're unsure about, and feels mediocre. Don't worry; we've got you covered! This chapter is all about transforming your writing into a work of art. Welcome to the Revision Revolution!

The Revision Process: A Step-by-Step Guide

Revamp your writing like a day at the spa: indulge your prose, polish rough patches, and sprinkle some magic.

Follow these steps to unleash your inner word wizard:

Step 1: The Time-Out Tonic: Put away your essay and take a break. Distance brings a fresh perspective, like admiring a clean kitchen after cooking.

Step 2: The Big-Picture Bird's Eye: "Get your favorite drink and start rereading your essay. Could you read it carefully and critically? Does it have a smooth flow like a TikTok transition? Are your arguments strong and effective, like a well-roasted meme? Is your conclusion a surprising twist or a boring and predictable end?"

Step 3: The Zoom-In Word Scrub: It's time to become laser-focused! You must eliminate clunky sentences, awkward phrases, or anything else that may need to be clarified for your reader. Remember, clarity is essential!

Step 4: The Grammar Gremlin Slayer: Avoid turning your writing into a grammar minefield by fixing pesky comma splices and misplaced apostrophes. While spellcheck can be helpful, it's not infallible like Gandalf the Wise. When in doubt, trust your instincts and consult a grammar guide. Remember, grammar mistakes are like annoying pop-up ads – confidently banish them!

Step 5: The Style Swagger Strut: "Your unique voice is your superpower! When you're writing, try reading your work aloud. Does it sound like you or like a textbook trying to be cool at a rooftop party? Make sure to inject your personality, sprinkle in some humor, and not be afraid to experiment with your language. Remember, your voice should shine like a disco ball in a dark room."

Editing for Clarity, Grammar, and Style: The Magical Trio

These are your secret ingredients for literary alchemy:

- **Clarity:** Imagine a laser beam directing your message. Each sentence should guide your readers along a clear path rather than leaving them in a confusing maze of jargon and metaphors. Strive for brevity, avoid rambling like a talkative grandma at Thanksgiving dinner, and explain complex ideas in ways your peers can easily comprehend.

- **Grammar**: Mastering grammar basics can feel like solving ancient riddles whispered by dusty scrolls, but once you do, it can make a significant difference in your writing. Punctuation is like a magic wand that can help you achieve a smooth flow of sentences and avoid confusion. Grammar mistakes can act like banana peels on your reader's path, so it's always a good idea to keep your spellcheck and dictionaries nearby.

- **Style:** Your personality sets you apart and makes your writing unique. Think of your writing style as a dance move entirely your own, and how you use words to create captivating stories and ideas makes you stand out. Don't be afraid to experiment with different sentence structures and tones to find your writing voice, and it's okay to use sarcasm if it helps you make your point. Always remember that the world needs your unique perspective and writing style.

- **Seeking Feedback: From Lone Wolf to Word Pack:** Share your work with trusted allies for valuable feedback. They can help you identify blind spots, suggest improvements, and celebrate your strengths. Be open-minded and choose your critics wisely, avoiding those who are overly pessimistic. Remember, feedback is a gift that helps you grow.

Examples

Imagine that you have written a persuasive essay advocating for later school start times. During the revision process, you might consider the following steps:

Step 1: Take a break, go to the park, and forget about school. This is especially important if you are writing about making school more fun. In that case, brainstorming in the park might be a great idea.

Step 2: Reread your essay and realize that while your arguments are strong, your conclusion feels as tired as a student who has just woken up after a 5 AM alarm.

Step 3: Rewrite the conclusion, adding a powerful call to action like "Let's ditch the zombie-eyed mornings and fuel our minds with sleep! Later start times, brighter minds, unite!"

Step 4: Check your grammar and spelling. Use a spell-checker and grammar guide to ensure your writing is free from typos and grammatical errors. Remember, good grammar is like an invisible bridge that connects your ideas and helps them flow smoothly.

Step 5: Read your essay aloud to your friends or classmates and ask for their feedback. Do you think your joke landing is going well? Is your tone engaging and conversational? Remember that your voice is your secret weapon, so use it confidently and let your personality shine through!

Bonus Challenge: "Create a revision checklist with your writing weaknesses and grammar errors. Use it to improve your writing quality and become a word wizard. "

Remember, revision isn't a punishment; it's a victory lap!

"Revise your writing to make it excellent and unique. Use practical tips like the comma wand and get feedback from peers. The Bonus Challenge encourages active participation. Embrace the revision process for better writing!"

🎯 ACTIVITY CORNER 8

Revision Challenge

Sample Essay:

Teenage Technology Takeover: In today's modern world, teenagers live in a constant vortex of technology. Screens dominate their lives, from phones permanently glued to their hands to endless hours lost in video game galaxies. This tech tsunami is drowning out essential aspects of teenage development, like face-to-face interaction and real-world experiences. We must act now to build dams against this digital deluge and protect our youth from its harmful effects.

First, teenagers glued to screens are missing out on crucial social skills. Talking to real people, forming eye contact, and navigating emotional cues in person are vital skills for adulthood. Yet, glued to screens, their communication muscles atrophy, leaving them socially awkward and unsure of themselves in real-world interactions. This can hinder their ability to build relationships, find jobs, and navigate the complexities of adult life.

Second, the endless digital content stream bombards teenagers with unrealistic expectations and shallow experiences. Social media feeds, filled with perfectly filtered selfies and curated experiences, create a distorted view of reality. Teenagers constantly compare their messy lives to these online highlight reels, leading to feelings of inadequacy, low self-esteem, and even depression. The constant stimulation of video games and instant gratification apps further desensitizes them to real-world experiences, making them crave excitement that may be unattainable in everyday life.

Finally, the tech takeover is chipping away at our teenagers' mental and physical health. The blue light emitted from screens disrupts sleep patterns, leading to fatigue, concentration issues, and even health problems in the long run. Additionally, hours spent hunched over devices can lead to poor posture, muscle weakness, and even an increased risk of obesity.

In conclusion, teenagers are drowning in a sea of technology, and we must throw them a lifeline. It's time to impose stricter limits on screen time, encourage alternative activities like sports and hobbies, and prioritize face-to-face interaction. Let's work together to ensure technology enhances their lives, not engulfs them.

What do you have to do?

Revise for clarity, grammar, and style. Make your arguments strong, your voice captivating, and your conclusion unforgettable. Unleash your inner editor and show the world the power of your revisions!

10. Practice Makes Perfect

Welcome to the chapter. You have learned valuable insights into essay writing; now it's time to apply those skills. This chapter focuses on improving your abilities through practical exercises, self-evaluation, and peer feedback.

Essay Prompts for Practice

Here are some writing prompts to help you improve your writing skills and spark your creativity. These prompts are diverse and are designed to challenge you in different ways. Take a look at them below:

- **Future Flashback**: Imagine you are living in a utopian or dystopian future. Write a letter to your past self, warning or celebrating the changes that await.

- **Unsung Hero**: Choose an everyday object or event and make it epic. Give a stapler its heroic monologue or tell the thrilling saga of a lost sock's journey through the laundry dryer.

- **Historical Remix**: Take a significant historical event and add a surprising twist. Imagine dinosaurs as Roman gladiators or witness the invention of the smartphone during the Renaissance.

- **Hidden Dimensions:** Explore the unseen sides of familiar things. Dive into the emotional world of your pet or uncover the philosophical musings of a dusty bookshelf in a forgotten corner.

- **Passion Project**: Analyze a topic you love through a unique lens. Explore the psychological appeal of rollercoasters, the poetic beauty of baking bread, or the surprising lessons learned from your favorite video game.

Self-Evaluation and Reflection: Hone Your Inner Critic

After completing each practice essay, it is essential to take a moment to reflect. Ask yourself the following questions:

- Were my arguments clear and well-structured?

- Was my thesis statement concise and compelling?

- Did I use evidence and examples effectively to support my arguments?

- Were my sentences well-written and free from grammatical errors?

- Did my unique voice come through in my writing in a way that engaged the reader?

- What did I learn as a result of writing this essay? Did it help me identify any areas for improvement or strengths that I can build on?

Remember, evaluating your writing is a great way to improve your skills and become a stronger writer.

Peer Review Exercises

Remember these tips when sharing your work with a writing partner. Peer review is not just about sharing your writing; it's about exchanging ideas with your partner. Follow these tips to provide constructive feedback:

1. **Blind Review**: Analyze the writing without revealing your names. Focus on clarity, grammar, and style like a keen observer.

2. **Strengths and Weaknesses**: Point out what you genuinely liked, followed by suggestions for improvement, like a gentle nudge in the right direction.

3. **Ask, Don't Tell**: Instead of dictating changes, pose questions encouraging your partner to reconsider and explore different options like a riddle.

4. **Be Respectful**: Feedback is a gift, not a weapon. Offer your opinions kindly and build each other up like true writing comrades.

🎯 ACTIVITY CORNER 9

Five-Paragraph Essay Arrangement Exercise: Decoding the Order

Here's an exercise to test your understanding of the five-paragraph essay structure:

Scenario: You have five paragraphs written for an essay, but they're out of order! Can you unscramble them and put them back in the correct sequence?

Prompts:

1. Each paragraph should have a distinct function in the essay structure. Identify the function of each paragraph based on its content and clues.
2. Consider the logical flow of ideas and how each paragraph builds upon the previous one.
3. Look for specific transitions or keywords that signal the order, like "Firstly," "However," or "In conclusion."

Challenge:

Arrange the following five paragraphs in the correct order for a persuasive essay arguing for shorter school days:

Paragraph A: Research indicates that teenagers require more sleep than adults. Shorter school days would allow them to get the rest they need, leading to improved cognitive function, focus, and overall well-being.

Paragraph B: Critics argue that shorter school days would hinder learning and academic achievement. However, studies show no significant decrease in academic performance with reduced school hours. Some students experience improved grades due to better focus and reduced stress.

Paragraph C: Think about it this way: imagine cramming eight hours of classes into six. The pace would be relentless, leaving students exhausted and struggling to retain information. Shorter school days, with more breaks and free time, would create a more effective learning environment.

Paragraph D: Imagine waking up at 6:00 am for six hours of classes. By lunchtime, many students are drained and disengaged. Longer school days don't necessarily translate to more effective learning.

Paragraph E: Therefore, it's time to prioritize student well-being and academic success by implementing shorter school days. This change would benefit students physically, mentally, and academically, ensuring they're well-rested, engaged, and prepared to learn their best.

ACTIVITY ANSWERS

ACTIVITY CORNER
SOLUTION

ACTIVITY 1

Answer to Paragraph Puzzle: "Unscramble the Wisdom of Sports"

Correct Paragraph Order:

(Paragraph D)
Exploring the connection between sports and mental well-being reveals a profound link between physical activity and psychological health. This connection is particularly evident in how sports reduce stress and improve mood.

(Paragraph A)
Sports contribute significantly to our mental well-being. Engaging in physical activities triggers the release of endorphins, the body's natural mood enhancers, positively impacting our mental state.

(Paragraph C)
The positive effects of sports on mental health extend beyond the physical aspect. Regular exercise has been linked to reduced symptoms of anxiety and depression, promoting a more balanced and resilient mind.

(Paragraph B)
Additionally, the camaraderie and social interactions fostered in sports environments create a sense of belonging and support, which is crucial in maintaining mental health.

(Paragraph E)
In conclusion, the holistic benefits of sports on mental health go beyond the physical realm. From stress reduction to enhanced mood and a sense of community, sports are vital in maintaining our overall mental well-being.

Reflection:
The arranged paragraphs now present a well-structured essay on "How Sports Helps in Our Mental Wellbeing," highlighting the interconnected aspects of physical activity, mental health, and the sense of community fostered by sports.

ACTIVITY CORNER
SOLUTION

ACTIVITY 2

1. **Analytical:**
"While social media platforms offer opportunities for connection and self-expression, their relentless curation of idealized body images has exacerbated body dissatisfaction and unhealthy comparisons among teens, leading to detrimental effects on mental health, self-esteem, and eating habits."

2. **Persuasive:**
"Learning a second language not only expands communication capabilities but also unlocks cognitive benefits, cultural understanding, and future career opportunities, making it an essential component of a well-rounded education that should be strongly encouraged in all academic institutions."

3. **Analytical:**
"Although often perceived as inherently challenging, growing up in a single-parent household can foster resilience, independence, and strong family bonds, challenging traditional assumptions about family structure and highlighting the importance of community support."

4. **Explanatory:**
"The ethical implications of artificial intelligence, from potential biases in decision-making to the replacement of human labor, demand careful consideration and comprehensive regulation to ensure its development aligns with societal values and prioritizes human well-being."

5. **Persuasive:**
"Music's ability to transcend language barriers, unite diverse communities, and shape individual and collective identities makes it a powerful tool for cultural understanding and social change, deserving greater recognition and support in educational and social settings."

ACTIVITY CORNER
SOLUTION

ACTIVITY 3

Paragraph 1: Sarah squinted at the chrome contraption, its metallic claws gleaming under the disco ball's light. Panic surged through her veins. What was this malfunctioning machine doing in her bedroom? Suddenly, the robot whirred to life, sparks leaping from its joints. A disembodied voice echoed, "Greetings, Sarah. I am Zorr, a time-traveling robot from the year 2247."
Transition: (c) In that instant,

Paragraph 2: Time travel? This had to be a joke. Zorr unfolded a holographic screen, displaying images of a futuristic cityscape bathed in neon lights. "Your world is in danger," the robot declared, his voice surprisingly gentle. Sarah's mind reeled. A time-traveling robot, a futuristic mission, danger... was this real?
Transition: (b) Consequently,

Paragraph 3: Sarah braced herself. "But I'm just a normal teenager!" she blurted, feeling fear and excitement. "You are the chosen one," Zorr insisted, his gaze unwavering. "A prophecy foretold that..." His words were cut short by a loud crash from downstairs. Sarah and Zorr exchanged startled glances. This was just the beginning.

Corrected Paragraph:

Sarah squinted at the chrome contraption, its metallic claws gleaming under the disco ball's light. Panic surged through her veins. What was this malfunctioning machine doing in her bedroom? The robot whirred to life instantly, sparks leaping from its joints. A disembodied voice echoed, "Greetings, Sarah. I am Zorr, a time-traveling robot from the year 2247."

Time travel? This had to be a joke. Zorr unfolded a holographic screen, displaying images of a futuristic cityscape bathed in neon lights. "Your world is in danger," the robot declared, his voice surprisingly gentle. Sarah's mind reeled.

ACTIVITY CORNER
SOLUTION

A time-traveling robot, a futuristic mission, danger... was this real? Consequently, Sarah braced herself. "But I'm just a normal teenager!" she blurted, feeling fear and excitement. "You are the chosen one," Zorr insisted, his gaze unwavering. "A prophecy foretold that..." His words were cut short by a loud crash from downstairs. Sarah and Zorr exchanged startled glances. This was just the beginning.

Remember, depending on interpretation and stylistic preference, there might be other "correct" solutions and transitions. Encourage your students to explore different options and justify their choices within the context of the paragraph's flow and logic.

I hope this activity with clear answers helps your students solidify their understanding of paragraph structure and transitions!

ACTIVITY 4

Essay Excerpt A: The Storyteller. The personal anecdote and connection to childhood memories highlight the emotional impact of the topic.

Essay Excerpt B: The Question Master. The thought-provoking question directly addresses the central debate of the essay, inviting the reader to consider different perspectives.

Essay Excerpt C: The Fact Fiend. The surprising statistic captures attention and establishes the essay's focus on the impact of the digital world.

Essay Excerpt D: The Scene Setter. The vivid imagery and sensory details transport the reader to the experience of travel, setting the stage for the essay's exploration of its transformational power.

Essay Excerpt E: The Quote Connoisseur. The powerful quote by Maya Angelou introduces the theme of storytelling and its significance, adding depth and authority to the essay's message.

Remember, these are just potential matches; the beauty of writing is that there's no one "correct" answer. Encourage students to consider their own preferences and the specific needs of their chosen topic when selecting an introduction style. The important thing is to craft an opening that effectively hooks the reader and sets the stage for a successful essay.

ACTIVITY CORNER SOLUTION

ACTIVITY 5

Unveiling the Essay Mystery: Matching Intros and Body Paragraphs!

After a thrilling investigation, it's time to reveal the perfect pairings for our Essay Matchmaker challenge:

Intro 1: Captivating Antiques - Body Paragraph C

Intro 2: The World of Online Gaming - Body Paragraph A

Intro 3: The Power of Food - Body Paragraph B

Intro 4: The Transformative Power of Reading - Body Paragraph D

Bonus Match: While not a perfect fit, Body Paragraph E (Baking Bread) could potentially connect with Intro 3 through the theme of food as a community builder. This pairing emphasizes the act of creation and sharing, highlighting the role food plays in bringing people together.

ACTIVITY 6

1. Time Warp to Contrast:
(b) In contrast,
Explanation: "Therefore" and "Consequently" imply that the previous point directly leads to longer breaks, which isn't quite the case. "For example" would be less effective for emphasis in a contrast situation.

2. Zoom Forward to Illustration:
(a) For instance,
Explanation: "Moreover" suggests further support for the general impact, while "Likewise" implies similarity, not illustration. "Hence" implies a cause-and-effect relationship, which isn't the intent here.

3. Flashback to Emphasis:
(b) Clearly,
Explanation: "As a result" implies a specific outcome of ignoring consequences, not emphasis on the urgency. "Similarly" wouldn't offer the necessary strength for this point. "On the other hand," presents a contrasting viewpoint, not the desired emphasis.

4. Fast Forward to Time Sequence:
(d) Next,
Explanation: "In fact" could connect but feels less natural for indicating time sequence. "Secondly" could work, but "Next" indicates moving forward within the narrative of technological evolution.

5. Rewind to Cause and Effect:
(c) Because,
Explanation: "Hence" could work but is slightly less direct for expressing cause and effect. The other options wouldn't connect reading to its broader impact on the individual.

ACTIVITY CORNER
SOLUTION

ACTIVITY 7

The BEST option is **Option 2**. Here's why:

- Emotional Impact: It uses vivid imagery and a conversational tone to connect with the reader personally.
- Call to Action: It empowers the reader with agency and encourages them to participate actively in the solution.
- Thought-provoking: It leaves a lingering question about individual responsibility and societal values.

While the other options offer valuable points, they lack the emotional depth and engaging call to action, making Option 2 the most effective conclusion for this essay.

Remember, the best conclusions are informative but also inspiring and memorable. They can spark change, raise awareness, and leave a lasting impression on your reader. Use your creativity, evoke emotions, and don't be afraid to take a stand!

ACTIVITY 8

Clarity:

Replace "teenagers live in a constant vortex of technology" with a more specific image, like "screens flicker like hypnotic flames before their eyes."
Instead of "their communication muscles atrophy," use a metaphor like "their conversation muscles turn to jelly under the digital sun."
Explain social media's "unrealistic expectations and shallow experiences" with concrete examples.

ACTIVITY CORNER
SOLUTION

ACTIVITY 9

Answer Key:
D, A, C, B, E

Explanation:

- **Paragraph D:** Starts with a vivid scenario, introducing the problem of long school days and student fatigue. This is a typical hook to capture the reader's attention.

- **Paragraph A:** Provides factual evidence and research to support the problem presented in D. This introduces the issue and thesis statement.

- **Paragraph C:** Uses an analogy and rhetorical question to explain the drawbacks of long school days further and argue for a different approach. This serves as a body paragraph with additional arguments.

- **Paragraph B:** Addresses potential counterarguments about academic impact and provides evidence to refute them. This is a counterargument paragraph showing the strength of the main argument.

- **Paragraph E:** Summarize the main points, reiterate the solution (shorter school days), and emphasize its benefits. This is the conclusion that leaves a lasting impression.

11. Ten Sample & Ten Practice Essays

SAMPLE ESSAY 1
SHOULD SOCIAL MEDIA PLATFORMS BE HELD RESPONSIBLE FOR HARMFUL CONTENT?

The internet has changed how we communicate, but it also has a dark side. Social media platforms are often filled with harmful content such as hate speech, cyberbullying, misinformation, and violent extremism. This raises the question of accountability: should companies like Facebook and Twitter be responsible for the content their users generate?

Opponents argue that holding platforms accountable would result in censorship and limit free speech. They believe it would lead to government intervention and suppressing opposing views, stifling online discourse and innovation. Additionally, platforms say it's impossible to monitor and remove all harmful material since a significant amount of user-generated content exists.

However, these arguments fail to recognize the real-world consequences of unchecked harmful content. The spread of misinformation has influenced elections and fueled social unrest. Hate speech and cyberbullying can have severe psychological effects on individuals, even leading to suicide. Platforms must not absolve themselves of responsibility since they profit from user engagement, even if it comes at the cost of human well-being.

Holding platforms accountable does not mean censorship. It means having clear-cut guidelines and proactive measures. Platforms must invest in content moderation algorithms and human review teams to identify and remove harmful material. They must also have transparent policies that outline their content moderation practices and hold themselves accountable for failures. Additionally, users should be empowered to report harmful content quickly and effectively.

In conclusion, social media platforms are potent tools for communication and connection. However, this power comes with a responsibility to ensure the safety and well-being of their users. While concerns about censorship are valid, they cannot hide the urgent need for accountability. By implementing effective content moderation practices, platforms can use their vast reach for good, creating a safer and more positive online environment for all.

Now below essay is similar in nature ,you can try to write!

PRACTICE ESSAY 1
SHOULD VIDEO GAME DEVELOPERS BE RESPONSIBLE FOR IN-GAME PURCHASES MADE BY MINORS?

SAMPLE ESSAY 2

DOES TECHNOLOGY CONTRIBUTE TO LONELINESS?

Technology has undeniably changed the way we interact with each other, from smartphones glued to our palms to endless digital distractions. While it boasts the potential to connect us with others across the globe, there is a growing concern that technology may make us lonelier.

Advocates of technology argue that social media platforms allow us to stay in touch with loved ones near and far, fostering connection and community. They also point out that online forums and gaming communities provide outlets for shared interests and virtual connections. Additionally, technology facilitates new forms of intimacy and understanding through real-time communication and emotional expression.

However, this optimistic view overlooks the detrimental impact of technology on real-world interactions. The constant buzz of notifications and screens can hinder meaningful face-to-face connection. We may be "friends" with hundreds online, but genuine, deep connections often suffer. Shallow interactions and fleeting digital exchanges leave gaps where authentic conversations and shared experiences used to be.

Moreover, technology can amplify the risk of loneliness and affect our psychological well-being. The curated, picture-perfect lives presented online can fuel envy and inadequacy, making us feel isolated and disconnected from our realities. The constant pressure to perform and "be seen" online can lead to anxiety and depression, further amplifying feelings of loneliness.

Technology, as a tool, is neither inherently good nor bad. It has the potential to bring us closer, but its misuse can easily lead to isolation. We must cultivate a mindful relationship with technology to combat the potential pitfalls. Setting boundaries, prioritizing real-world interactions, and engaging in offline activities are crucial. We must remember that genuine connection comes not from a screen but from shared experiences and authentic conversations with those who truly matter.

Now below essay is similar in nature ,you can try to write!

PRACTICE ESSAY 2

DOES THE CONSTANT PURSUIT OF "PERFECT" ONLINE PERSONAS DAMAGE SELF-ESTEEM?

SAMPLE ESSAY 3
SHOULD LOCAL DIALECTS AND ACCENTS BE ENCOURAGED OR STANDARDIZED IN EDUCATION?

Language is a complex tapestry that weaves history, culture, and identity together. It comprises diverse strands, including local dialects and accents that add texture and nuance. However, when it comes to education, the question arises: should language standardization be a priority, or should we celebrate the uniqueness of these variations?

Those who advocate for standardization believe that a uniform language is necessary for effective communication and academic success. They argue that dialects and accents can create barriers to understanding and limit student opportunities. Standardized language provides clarity and coherence, giving students a shared platform for learning and access to higher education. Additionally, proponents of standardization believe that promoting dialects weakens the development of critical literacy skills required for advanced studies.

On the other hand, supporters of embracing dialectal diversity assert that local languages are not obstacles but rather markers of identity and cultural heritage. Suppressing them can lead to feelings of alienation and erode the richness of language itself. Dialects offer unique perspectives and expressions, enriching the learning experience and fostering tolerance for linguistic diversity. Furthermore, studies have shown that suppressing dialects can hinder cognitive development and creativity in children.

Finding a harmonious balance is essential. Educational systems can promote standard grammar and vocabulary while acknowledging and appreciating the value of local dialects. Encouraging code-switching, where students navigate between dialects and the standard form, can equip them with the linguistic versatility necessary for various social and professional settings. This approach empowers students to claim their cultural identities while preparing them for broader communication.

Teachers can also incorporate local dialects and accents into the curriculum. Analyzing regional literature, studying the history of language variations, and encouraging creative writing in native dialects can deepen students' understanding of their language and foster appreciation for linguistic diversity. This can break down stereotypes and build bridges between different communities within the school environment.

Ultimately, the focus should shift from standardization as a one-size-fits-all solution to fostering linguistic awareness and inclusivity. Embracing the tapestry of language, with its standardized threads and vibrant dialectal hues, allows us to nurture effective communication and cultural pride within our educational systems. By doing so, we create a more prosperous learning environment that celebrates the diverse voices and identities that make up our society.

Now below essay is similar in nature ,you can try to write!

PRACTICE ESSAY 3

SHOULD LOCAL DIALECTS AND ACCENTS BE ENCOURAGED OR STANDARDIZED IN EDUCATION?

SAMPLE ESSAY 4

THE ETHICAL IMPLICATIONS OF ARTIFICIAL INTELLIGENCE

Artificial Intelligence (AI) promises a future of technological wonders, from self-driving cars to automated surgeons. However, with every leap forward, ethical questions also arise. The power AI wields, its susceptibility to bias, and its potential impact on humanity demands careful consideration as we navigate this uncharted territory.

One of the most pressing concerns is the concentration of power. As AI algorithms become more sophisticated, they take on tasks that were once done only by humans. This raises the possibility of AI algorithms wielding unchecked power, perpetuating existing biases, or making opaque and unaccountable decisions. For example, an AI judge sentencing a defendant based on incomplete or biased data or societal prejudices encoded within its programming. Such scenarios can become a chilling reality if we fail to address the ethical concerns surrounding power imbalances.

AI has inherent biases because algorithms are trained on human-created datasets that reflect societal inequalities. This can lead to discrimination in everything from recruitment to facial recognition. We need active mitigation strategies like diversified datasets and rigorous bias detection algorithms to reduce AI's potential to amplify existing inequalities.

Finally, the long-term impact of AI on humanity raises questions about our future. As AI becomes more intelligent and autonomous, we may face a future where machines surpass human capabilities in every domain. This raises questions about our identity, purpose, and role in a world dominated by artificial intelligence. Will we become obsolete cogs in a machine-driven world, or can we forge a symbiotic relationship with AI that leverages its power for the betterment of humanity?

In conclusion, the ethical implications of AI are not some distant dystopian prospect but pressing questions that require immediate attention. From grappling with power imbalances and mitigating bias to ensuring a future where humans and AI co-exist harmoniously, we must work together to pave the ethical roadmap for AI development. By prioritizing transparency, accountability, and a nuanced understanding of the potential pitfalls, we can navigate the ethical minefield of AI and ensure that this transformative technology serves humanity's progress, not its demise.

Now below essay is similar in nature, you can try to write!

PRACTICE ESSAY 4

HOW WILL AUTOMATION IN THE WORKPLACE AFFECT FUTURE JOB OPPORTUNITIES?

SAMPLE ESSAY 5

THE IMPACT OF GLOBALIZATION ON CULTURAL IDENTITY

Globalization is the term used to describe our world as it is now. It is a world where countries are connected, and information flows freely like electricity. Cultures worldwide are now coming into contact with each other, like bumper cars in a digital amusement park. But, for teenagers, navigating this world can be confusing. They wonder how globalization affects their cultural identity.

At first glance, globalization opens up endless possibilities. Teenagers are exposed to various music, from K-pop to Bollywood, and decorate their rooms with posters and art from different countries. They wear clothes from China and enjoy food worldwide while chatting with friends from different countries on video calls. This cultural buffet exposes teenagers to different perspectives, breaks down geographic barriers, and makes the world feel like their playground. Thanks to globalization, they can explore different cultures and build a unique identity made up of influences from around the world.

Our world is connected, so we're exposed to different cultures daily. However, this can sometimes lead to confusion about our cultural identity. We may be stuck between our family traditions and the latest trends and feel like we're losing touch with our roots.

To navigate this maze, we need to find balance. We should embrace the diverse world around us and let it inspire us. We can try new things, like learning a new language or dish. But we should also remember our roots and continue to hold onto the traditions and stories that connect us to our past.

Our cultural identity is a work in progress. It's a dance between our heritage and the world around us. We should be open to new experiences and perspectives and remember who we are and where we come from. We can create a unique identity grounded in our roots and connected to our world.

In summary, we should embrace the richness of globalization while staying true to ourselves. We should be open to new things but also remember our roots. Our cultural identity is the pearl we create within the world. So, let's explore, learn, share, and most importantly, be ourselves – global citizens with deep and broad roots.

Now below essay is similar in nature ,you can try to write!

PRACTICE ESSAY 5

HOW CAN WE MAINTAIN LOCAL TRADITIONS WHILE EMBRACING A GLOBALIZED WORLD?

SAMPLE ESSAY 6
THE RISE OF "FAKE NEWS" AND ITS THREAT TO DEMOCRACY.

Imagine a world where the news you read is like a funhouse mirror, distorting reality and twisting facts. Fake news is misleading information that spreads quickly on social media. It can be harmful and affect our way of thinking. It can even influence important decisions, like elections.

Fake news is often designed to appeal to our emotions. Sometimes, it takes work to distinguish between real and fake news. But it's essential to be aware of it and to check facts before sharing anything. You can verify the news source and ensure it's reliable.

Fake news can have serious consequences. It can affect people's lives and careers. It can also create social unrest and change the way we see different groups of people. We must be careful about what we share and ensure accurate information.

To combat fake news, we need to be informed and alert. Check the source of the news. It probably is if it sounds too good (or bad) to be true. Report fake news when you see it and spread awareness among your friends and family. Remember, every click on a fake news story or every share of a misleading meme fuels the problem. We can all play a part in being the digital superhero who fights for truth and holds misinformation accountable.

Ultimately, it's up to every single one of us to combat fake news. By educating ourselves, being critical information consumers, and actively working to spread truth, we can protect our democracies from the shadows of deception. So, the next time you see a suspicious headline, remember: you have the power to break the chain, to be the truth warrior who clicks back against the tide of fake news.

In conclusion, social media platforms are potent tools for communication and connection. However, this power comes with a responsibility to ensure the safety and well-being of their users. While concerns about censorship are valid, they cannot hide the urgent need for accountability. By implementing effective content moderation practices, platforms can use their vast reach for good, creating a safer and more positive online environment for all.

Now below essay is similar in nature ,you can try to write!

PRACTICE ESSAY 6

HOW CAN INDIVIDUALS DEVELOP CRITICAL THINKING SKILLS TO NAVIGATE AN INFORMATION-SATURATED WORLD?

SAMPLE ESSAY 7
THE CHALLENGES AND OPPORTUNITIES OF CLIMATE CHANGE.

Okay, let's be honest: climate change can seem scary. Melting glaciers, raging wildfires, and strange weather patterns can make you want to hide under your bed and watch a dystopian movie (but that's not a great idea). However, there are opportunities to be found amidst the challenges.

The challenges are real. Rising sea levels threaten coastal communities, extreme weather events disrupt lives and livelihoods, and the changing climate throws ecosystems into disarray. But we can be the engineers who build a new, eco-friendly world.

Here's the exciting part: Imagine a world powered by the sun and wind, where electric cars are the norm, and cities are green with rooftop gardens and vertical farms. Imagine jobs in renewable energy, eco-tourism, and green tech, with companies competing to invent the next best climate-saving gadget. Climate change can catalyze a global innovation boom, creating new industries and empowering us to be the ultimate problem-solvers.

Think about it: even as a teenager with a smartphone and a head of ideas, you could be the next climate hero. You could invent a device that captures CO_2 from the air, design a sustainable fashion line, or even spearhead a community project to reduce waste. The possibilities are endless, and your voice matters. Remember Greta Thunberg? She started at 15, skipping school to protest climate inaction. Now, she's inspiring millions and holding world leaders accountable.

So, don't just picture dystopian landscapes next time you hear about climate change. Picture a world where clean air is a luxury, not a privilege, where innovation thrives, and where we, the young generation, are at the forefront of building a better future.

Climate change is a challenge, but it's also an opportunity to rewrite the story, to prove that humans aren't just good at messing things up and fixing them in the most incredible, innovative ways possible. So, buckle up, get ready for the ride, and let's turn this climate rollercoaster into a green revolution!

Now below essay is similar in nature, you can try to write!

PRACTICE ESSAY 7

CAN SMALL, INDIVIDUAL ACTIONS MAKE A SIGNIFICANT DIFFERENCE IN ENVIRONMENTAL PROTECTION?

SAMPLE ESSAY 8
THE ETHICAL DILEMMAS OF SPACE EXPLORATION.

Imagine flying through space, leaving Earth behind as you reach for the stars. Space exploration is exciting, with the promise of scientific discoveries and the possibility of finding life beyond our planet. But before starting this cosmic journey, we must consider some important ethical questions.

The first question is about resources. Every rocket launch and satellite sent into space uses many of our planet's resources. Is it right to prioritize space exploration when so many people on Earth don't have access to basic needs? We must balance exploring space and caring for our planet and its inhabitants.

Another question is about the environment. Rockets emit gases that contribute to climate change. Should we continue polluting our planet while we look for other planets to live on? We need to find ways to explore space while also protecting our planet.

However, space exploration can also bring benefits. It can lead to technological advancements that improve life on Earth, such as medical breakthroughs and better weather forecasting. And who knows, we might find evidence of life beyond our planet, which would be a significant discovery that could unite us all.

The ethical questions around space exploration are complex, and there is no easy answer. But we can have open and honest discussions about these issues, ensuring that our curiosity about space balances our responsibility to our planet and its people. We must remember that everyone should benefit from space exploration and not leave anyone behind.

Now below essay is similar in nature, you can try to write!

PRACTICE ESSAY 8

SHOULD RESOURCES BE INVESTED IN SPACE EXPLORATION WHILE FACING SOCIAL AND ENVIRONMENTAL PROBLEMS ON EARTH?

SAMPLE ESSAY 9

THE GROWING INFLUENCE OF CELEBRITY CULTURE.

From the red carpet glow to Instagram stories dripping with FOMO, celebrities seem to rule the world nowadays. From pop stars to influencers, their faces plaster billboards, their outfits inspire trends, and their every sneeze trends on Twitter. But hold on, teens, before you get swept up in the celebrity whirlwind, let's take a step back and decode this cultural phenomenon.

First, why are we so obsessed anyway? It's like a magic trick. Celebrities are these larger-than-life figures living seemingly perfect lives, surrounded by luxury and fame. They're the ultimate escape from our

everyday routines, a constant dose of excitement and drama on a silver platter. Plus, they tap into our need to belong, offering a sense of community through fandoms and shared obsessions. We stand, our faves, feeling part of something bigger than ourselves.

But here's the catch: what you see on social media and magazines is only part of the story. Celebrities are brands with meticulously crafted personalities designed to sell products and influence trends. It's easy to get blinded by the airbrushed photos and carefully curated online personas, forgetting that celebrities are humans with insecurities and imperfections. Chasing unrealistic beauty standards or constantly comparing your life to theirs can be a recipe for low self-esteem and anxiety.

So, how do we navigate this world of curated fame without losing ourselves in the glitz and glamour? The key is to be a critical consumer of celebrity culture. Don't just unquestioningly worship every trend or buy into every hype. Ask yourself: why am I attracted to this celebrity? What message are they sending? Do I genuinely admire their talent or their lifestyle? Remember, you are the star of your own story, not a supporting character in someone else's.

Celebrity culture can be fun, but it shouldn't define our values or dictate our goals. Instead, use it as inspiration, not aspiration. Find your passions, cultivate your talents, and create your version of success. Remember, your story is waiting to be written, and it's guaranteed to be way more interesting than any airbrushed Instagram feed. So, keep your eyes on the prize – your unique path to shine brighter than any celebrity spotlight.

Now below essay is similar in nature ,you can try to write!

PRACTICE ESSAY 9

SHOULD WE ADMIRE CELEBRITIES FOR THEIR TALENTS OR SCRUTINIZE THEIR PERSONAL LIVES?

SAMPLE ESSAY 10

THE POWER OF MUSIC TO TRANSCEND BORDERS AND CULTURES.

Do you ever feel like music can transport you to another world? Music is a universal language that connects people worldwide, regardless of their culture or language. Music is more important than ever in today's diverse and interconnected world, especially for teenagers like you.

Music can break down walls between people. A catchy melody or an awesome guitar riff can bring you together even if you don't speak the same language. Shared musical experiences can create a bond and help you understand others better.

Music can also inspire curiosity. A song can take you on a journey to a new and different world, introducing you to different cultures, traditions, and stories. Each song is like a treasure waiting to be discovered, offering a peek into a different way of life.

Music can also be a powerful tool for change. Throughout history, music has been used to promote social and political movements. Teenagers can use music to raise awareness, challenge injustice, and inspire change.

Finally, music can create a sense of belonging. Whether at a concert or singing karaoke with friends, music can bring people together and create a sense of community. It allows us to connect with others who share our interests and passions, reminding us that we're not alone in the world.

So, next time you listen to music, remember that it's more than just a song. It's a way to break down barriers, explore new worlds, inspire change, and create a sense of belonging. Turn up the volume, open your ears, and let the music take you on a journey.

Now below essay is similar in nature ,you can try to write!

PRACTICE ESSAY 10

HOW DOES MUSIC REFLECT AND INFLUENCE SOCIAL MOVEMENTS AND POLITICAL CHANGE?

12. Prompt Challenge

PROMPT CHALLENGE

Reflective Essay Prompt:
- Activity: Reflect on a significant moment in your life. Write a reflective essay using the 5-paragraph structure to explore the impact of that moment on your personal growth.

Debating Perspectives Prompt:
- Activity: Choose a current social issue and write a 5-paragraph essay presenting two perspectives. Explore the arguments for each viewpoint.

Book Review Prompt:
- Activity: Read a book you recently enjoyed. Write a book review using the 5-paragraph essay structure. Discuss the plot, characters, and your overall recommendation.

Personal Passion Prompt:
- Activity: Identify a hobby or passion of yours. Write an essay exploring why this activity is meaningful to you, using personal anecdotes and examples.

Future Aspirations Prompt:
- Activity: Imagine your life ten years from now. Write a 5-paragraph essay outlining your future aspirations, career goals, and the steps you plan to take to achieve them.

Analyzing a Quote Prompt:
- Activity: Choose a meaningful quote and write an essay analyzing its significance. Explore how the quote relates to your life or to broader societal themes.
  1.

Historical Event Exploration Prompt:
- Activity: Select a historical event that interests you. Write an essay discussing the event's causes, effects, and long-term impacts on society.

Technology's Impact Prompt:
- Activity: Explore the impact of technology on modern life. Write an essay discussing technology's positive and negative effects, using specific examples.

Character Analysis Prompt:
- Activity: Choose a character from a book, movie, or TV show. Write an essay analyzing the character's traits, motivations, and role in the narrative.

Environmental Awareness Prompt:
- Activity: Investigate an environmental issue that concerns you. Write a 5-paragraph essay discussing the causes, consequences, and potential solutions related to that issue.

CONCLUSION

Dear young writers, congratulations! You have completed the 5-paragraph Essay Blueprint workbook successfully. You have learned how to structure your essays, write compelling paragraphs, and use words to express your thoughts.

This workbook is just the beginning of your writing journey. You have the power to share your unique voice with the world and make an impact with your writing.

Remember to revise your work, use transitions, and write a convincing conclusion. The writing exercises in this workbook can help you continue to grow and improve your writing skills.

Writing is a lifelong adventure, so enjoy the process, embrace the blank page, and allow your words to take flight.

You have the potential to change the world with your writing, so keep writing bravely and boldly. We believe in you!

OTHER BOOKS